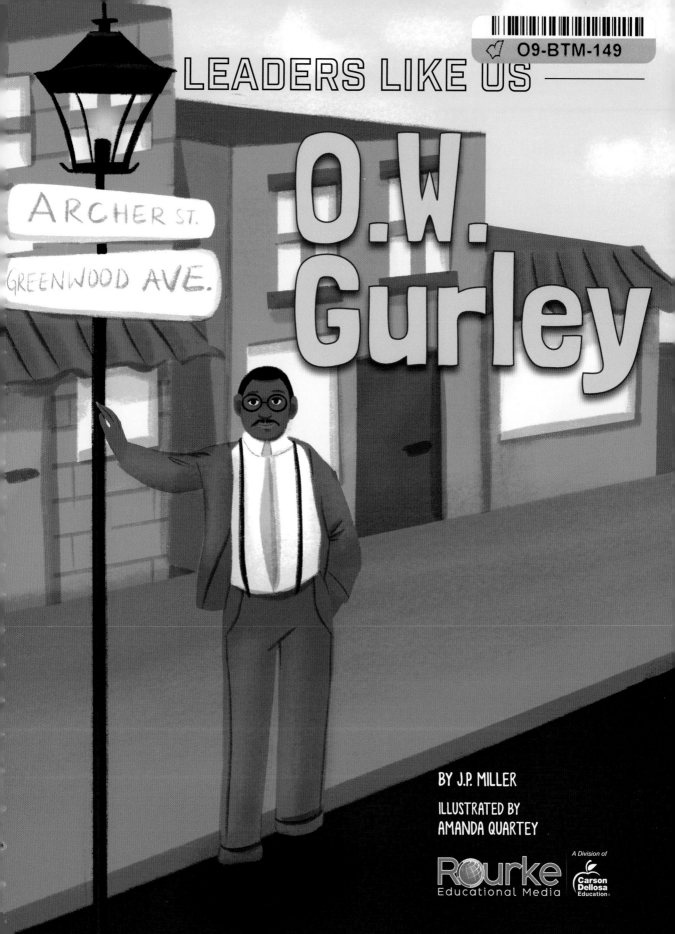

LEADERS LIKE US

O.W. Gurley

BY J.P. MILLER

ILLUSTRATED BY
AMANDA QUARTEY

Rourke
Educational Media

A Division of
Carson
Dellosa
Education

ROURKE'S
SCHOOL to HOME
CONNECTIONS
BEFORE AND DURING READING ACTIVITIES

Before Reading: *Building Background Knowledge and Vocabulary*

Building background knowledge can help children process new information and build upon what they already know. Before reading a book, it is important to tap into what children already know about the topic. This will help them develop their vocabulary and increase their reading comprehension.

Questions and Activities to Build Background Knowledge:

1. Look at the front cover of the book and read the title. What do you think this book will be about?
2. What do you already know about this topic?
3. Take a book walk and skim the pages. Look at the table of contents, photographs, captions, and bold words. Did these text features give you any information or predictions about what you will read in this book?

Vocabulary: *Vocabulary Is Key to Reading Comprehension*

Use the following directions to prompt a conversation about each word.

- Read the vocabulary words.
- What comes to mind when you see each word?
- What do you think each word means?

> **Vocabulary Words:**
> - *commercial*
> - *employee*
> - *employer*
> - *entrepreneur*
> - *invest*
> - *loans*
> - *residential*
> - *wealth*

During Reading: *Reading for Meaning and Understanding*

To achieve deep comprehension of a book, children are encouraged to use close reading strategies. During reading, it is important to have children stop and make connections. These connections result in deeper analysis and understanding of a book.

Close Reading a Text

During reading, have children stop and talk about the following:

- Any confusing parts
- Any unknown words
- Text to text, text to self, text to world connections
- The main idea in each chapter or heading

Encourage children to use context clues to determine the meaning of any unknown words. These strategies will help children learn to analyze the text more thoroughly as they read.

When you are finished reading this book, turn to the next-to-last page for **Text-Dependent Questions** and an **Extension Activity**.

TABLE OF CONTENTS

BUILDING A COMMUNITY

   Do you want to work and make money? What job do you want to do? Do you want to be the **employer** or the **employee**? Ottawa (O.W.) Gurley was an employer. He was a leader in business.

As far as the eye could see there were oil wells. It was the oil boom of 1905. This is what brought O.W. and many others to Tulsa, Oklahoma. He was ready to start a new life. He wanted to be part of building a community.

O.W. looked for the best land. He wanted to buy it to sell later. He bought 40 acres on the city's north side. He designated some land **commercial** and some **residential**. He made it clear that his land was only to be sold to Black people.

ROOMING HOUSE

The first business O.W. started on the north side was a rooming house; a house with multiple rooms that were rented out to people individually. Then, he opened a grocery store. This was the beginning of the Greenwood Community. It became one of the wealthiest Black communities in America. It earned the name "Black Wall Street."

THE GREENWOOD COMMUNITY

Greenwood was home to around 10,000 Black people during the 1920s. The community thrived with successful businesses and elite schools that prepared students for higher education.

RACE TO
CLAIM

Some believe a child born on Christmas Day is special. That was true of O.W. He was born on December 25, 1868. His parents were John and Rosanna Gurley. They were former enslaved people.

By age 21, O.W. had married his childhood sweetheart, Emma Wells. O.W. wasn't always an **entrepreneur**. Before he became a business leader, he worked as a teacher and for the U.S. Postal Service. He always looked for ways to better himself and others.

O.W. was very smart. He went to public schools for a while. But most of what he learned about business was on his own. He worked hard. He learned to **invest** his money. He became one of the wealthiest Black men in America.

In 1889, Oklahoma had its first land rush. It was a race to claim land. O.W. heard about the free land and packed up everything. He and Emma moved west. He was determined to get some land.

The land O.W. claimed was part of what would later be named Perry, Oklahoma. He ran for County Treasurer but lost. Instead, he was chosen to be the school principal. The first business he opened was a general store. O.W. and Emma lived in Perry until 1905, when O.W. heard about the oil fields making people rich in Tulsa. He sold his land and moved 80 miles east.

THE OKLAHOMA LAND RUSH OF 1889

Modern-day Oklahoma was once called Indian Territory. The government had forced American Indians, such as the Chickasaw, Choctaw, Cherokee, Creek, Cheyenne, Commanche, and Apache, out of their traditional lands and relocated them to Indian Territory. Eventually, the government took sections of this land as well and offered it to new settlers. People rushed to claim this land as their own.

O.W.'s 40 acres of land were on the north side of Tulsa. A line divided the citizens of Tulsa. It could not be missed. It was the train tracks. Black people lived on the north side of the tracks in the area they named Greenwood. White people filled out the rest of the city. Black people were only allowed to cross the tracks for work or other specific business.

O.W. helped Greenwood thrive. He sold land to Black families. He made loans to Black entrepreneurs who promised to build up Greenwood with him. Together they built the things needed for their community.

They founded churches . . .
made recreation spaces . . .
and, started small businesses.

The people of Greenwood were doing great.

15

PERFUME

JEWELER

REST

Booker T. Washington
visited Tulsa. He was
surprised by the **wealth**
of the Greenwood
Community. He
nicknamed the area
"Black Wall Street."

Not everyone was happy about the thriving Black community. Many white people were jealous. They did not want Black people to have a lot of money. They were angry at the success of Greenwood.

BOOKER T. WASHINGTON

Booker T. Washington was born an enslaved person but was freed by the Emancipation Proclamation. He rose to be one of the most influential voices of his time. Washington was an author, educator, and advisor to several American presidents.

One day, their anger turned to rage. A Black man was falsely accused of attacking a white woman. The white residents of Tulsa used the incident as an excuse to attack. A group of white people set fire to Greenwood. They burned houses and businesses. They murdered hundreds of Black people. Greenwood was destroyed.

Everything O.W. helped build was gone. He and Emma moved to Los Angeles, California, to start over. There, he owned another rooming house and worked in politics. O.W. died on August 6, 1935.

In October 1995, the Greenwood Cultural Center opened. It is still working to preserve, honor, and celebrate Greenwood's history. O.W. was honored in the 2009 film; *Before They Die! The True Story of the Survivors of the 1921 Tulsa Race Riot and Their Quest for Justice*. May 2021 marked the 100-year anniversary of the Tulsa Race Massacre.

> " Greenwood shows that when we are left to our own devices and don't have a knee to our neck, we can achieve extraordinary things. "
>
> —John W. Rogers Jr., the great-grandson of J.B. Stradford, a fellow Greenwood entrepreneur.

TIME LINE

1868   O.W. Gurley is born December 25th in Huntsville, Alabama but is raised in Pine Bluff, Arkansas.

1889   O.W. Gurley marries Emma Wells on November 6th.

1889   O.W. Gurley participates in the Oklahoma Land Rush. Claims land in Perry.

1905   O.W. Gurley sells Perry, Oklahoma, property and moves 80 miles east to homestead in Tulsa.

1905   O.W. Gurley purchases 40 acres of land and establishes the Greenwood Community in Tulsa. The community is nicknamed "Black Wall Street."

1905   O.W. Gurley establishes his first business in Greenwood—a rooming house.

1921   The Tulsa Race Massacre takes place from May 31st to June 1st. Over 300 Black residents are killed.

1921   O.W. and Emma Gurley move to Los Angeles, California following the Tulsa Race Massacre.

1935   O.W. Gurley dies in Los Angeles, California, on August 6th.

1995   Greenwood Cultural Center is established October 22nd.

2009   O.W. Gurley is honored in the documentary film; *Before They Die! The True Story of the Survivors of the 1921 Tulsa Race Riot and Their Quest for Justice.*

2021   Greenwood memorializes the 100th anniversary of the Tulsa Race Massacre.

GLOSSARY

commercial (kuh-MUR-shuhl): of or having to do with buying and selling things

employee (em-PLOI-ee): a person who is paid to work for another person or business

employer (em-PLOY-ur): a person or company that pays people to work for them

entrepreneur (ahn-truh-pruh-NUR): someone who starts businesses and finds new ways to make money

invest (in-VEST): to give or lend money to something, such as a company, with the intention of getting more money back later

loans (lohnz): the act of lending something to someone, especially money

residential (rez-i-DEN-shuhl): of or having to do with a neighborhood or an area where people live

wealth (welth): a great amount of money, property, or valuable possessions

INDEX

TEXT-DEPENDENT QUESTIONS

1. What was the Oklahoma Land Rush of 1889?
2. Why was the Greenwood Community called Black Wall Street?
3. What was the first business started by O.W. Gurley?
4. How much land did O.W. Gurley buy when he arrived in Tulsa, Oklahoma?
5. Where did O.W. Gurley move to when he left Tulsa?

EXTENSION ACTIVITY

Imagine you are going to start a business of your own. Decide what kind of business you want to run. What are you going to sell? Make up a company name and slogan. Create your own advertisement for your company on a computer or on a sheet of paper. Show your products and prices on the advertisement.

ABOUT THE AUTHOR

J.P. Miller Growing up, J.P. Miller loved reading stories that she could become immersed in. As a writer, she enjoys doing the same for her readers. Through the gift of storytelling, she is able to bring little- and well-known people and events in African American history to life for young readers. She hopes that her stories will augment the classroom experience and inspire her readers. J.P. lives in metro Atlanta and is the author of the *Careers in the US Military* and *Black Stories Matter* series. J.P. is the winner of the 2021 Black Authors Matter Award sponsored by the National Black Book Festival.

ABOUT THE ILLUSTRATOR

Amanda Quartey Amanda lives in the UK and was born and bred in London. She has always loved to draw and has been doing so ever since she can remember. At the age of 14, she moved to Ghana and studied art in school. She later returned to the UK to study graphic design. Her artistic path deviated slightly when she studied Classics at her university. Over the years, in a bid to return to her artistic roots, Amanda has built a professional illustration portfolio and is now loving every bit of her illustration career.

www.rourkeeducationalmedia.com

Quote source: Gara, Antoine. "The Baron of Black Wall Street," Forbes, May 31, 2021: https://www.forbes.com/sites/antoinegara/2020/06/18/the-bezos-of-black-wall-street-tulsa-race-riots-1921/?sh=3a391eaaf321.

Edited by: Hailey Scragg
Illustrations by: Amanda Quartey
Cover and interior layout by: J.J. Giddings

Library of Congress PCN Data

O.W. Gurley / J.P. Miller
(Leaders Like Us)
ISBN 978-1-73165-181-5 (hard cover)
ISBN 978-1-7316-5226-3 (soft cover)
ISBN 978-1-73165-196-9 (e-Book)
ISBN 978-1-73165-211-9 (ePub)
Library of Congress Control Number: 2021944584

Rourke Educational Media
Printed in the United States of America
01-3402111937